SETTING THE TABLE

The Tenant's Guide

to

Understanding and Negotiating

the

Restaurant Lease

ALAN D. ARONSON

Dedication

to my parents, Gloria and Bob,
for giving me the tools

and

to my wife, Robin,
for inspiring me to use them

ISBN-13: 978-1500606749

ISBN-10: 150060674X

Acknowledgments

This book would not exist without the support of Mary Scibello, who managed my law practice for twenty years, and who labored over numerous drafts of the manuscript.

I am grateful for the editorial assistance provided by Margaret Petersen, one of the country's most experienced retail leasing attorneys.

I thank Steven Mannheim for his comments on the manuscript and for his encouragement.

Contents

Introduction   i

Chapter One: The Basic Restaurant Lease   1

Chapter Two: Restaurants in Shopping Centers   12

Chapter Three: Restaurants in Mixed-Use Projects   20

Chapter Four: Restaurants in Hotels   24

Chapter Five: Drive-Thru Restaurants   30

Conclusion   32

Appendix A: Letter of Intent   33

Appendix B: Work Letter   39

Appendix C: Construction Timeline   43

Appendix D: CAM Exclusions   45

Introduction

It takes a lot of work to open a restaurant. It takes even more work, and some luck, to keep it open. Many restaurants fail during the first few years of operation. As long as you have time, you should position yourself for success, both in the kitchen and on paper. Your lease is a great place to start. Many challenges of operating a restaurant relate to the use and maintenance of the leased space. When a problem arises, tenants are often surprised to find that their lease fails to provide a practical remedy, or worse, fails to address the problem at all. This book guides you through issues that are unique to restaurant leases and offers practical advice on crafting remedies that can be enforced quickly and with a minimum of expense.

This distinguished professor will appear throughout the book to offer advice based on his many years of studying the food service business.

Introductory Lecture: "But He Seems So Nice..." Are you thinking you don't need this book because your landlord is "nice?" Check, please . . . and here is your tip: during the lease term, your nice landlord may sell the building to someone who is not so nice, or your landlord may simply turn out to be less friendly than you expected. Recently, the owner of a successful restaurant spent a fortune renovating the premises. The restaurant's lease had expired many years earlier, but the "nice landlord" kept extending the lease term at the same rent. What do you think happened after the landlord's son assumed control of the property and learned of the tenant's expensive renovations? The answer is in the book, but I'll bet you can guess. (Hint: The son was not quite as nice as his father.)

Restaurant management teams often give only cursory attention to the lease. Reading legal documents is not as interesting as planning a menu and interviewing chefs. Menus can be revised and chefs can be replaced, but you will have to live with your lease for a long time, so you should make an effort to understand the benefits it provides and the restrictions it imposes. Once you open for business, the day-to-day struggle for survival will consume most of your time, and you will find yourself juggling many problems. Some of these problems (such as a leaking roof or a broken air conditioning unit) may be expensive to fix, and, if not promptly repaired, may cause damage to your improvements or result in the loss of business. It is at such moments that you will pull your lease out of the file cabinet and, with fingers crossed, look for language that requires the landlord to pay the repair costs or that provides some other helpful remedy. Given the enormous expense of opening and operating a restaurant, and the relentless competition and thin profit margins prevalent in the industry, it often takes only a minor miscalculation or a bit of bad luck to reduce a successful enterprise to an empty storefront. Many things that go wrong are outside the operator's control, but the restaurant's lease should address as many issues as possible.

The Light Bulb indicates a "bright idea" that will save time or money.

Introductory Bright Idea: The Recycled Lease. To reduce legal fees, ask your landlord if the first draft of the lease can be based on an existing lease for another restaurant similar in style, size and location.

Because most books about retail leasing do not distinguish between restaurants and general retail businesses, they overlook important issues unique to restaurant leases. This book focuses on provisions that should be in a restaurant lease, and the modifications to a typical commercial lease form that are appropriate for restaurants in different settings. Don't be fooled into thinking that the document presented to you by the landlord as the "standard form" that "all tenants sign" is fair, reasonable, or complete; all leases are drafted in favor of the person presenting them, and all leases can and should be negotiated.

The Scales of Justice indicate an explanation of a legal concept or issue.

Introductory Issue: "You Must Pay the Rent." "I Can't Pay the Rent." "I'll Pay the Rent." "My Hero." Do you know that a subtenant that pays its rent on time and does everything else required under its sublease can still be evicted? Do you know how to prevent this? Keep reading.

This book assumes no particular level of experience with leases and is written for a broad audience, from readers who are new to the restaurant industry and need to learn the basics of leasing, to those who already operate a restaurant and want to better understand their lease, to anyone who is simply curious about the business of operating a restaurant. If you are directly involved in negotiating a restaurant lease, then the information presented in this book will help you take control of the leasing process and become a knowledgeable participant able to evaluate a range of available options and make informed decisions.

The Legal Stuff. Although the author is a licensed attorney, this book is intended solely as an educational resource. No attorney-client relationship is created by the purchase of this book. The author is not offering legal advice, and no statement is to be taken as correctly or completely setting forth the law of any particular jurisdiction or the effect of including or not including any particular language or concept in a lease. Laws and their interpretations, and commercial real estate leasing customs and practices, vary from state to state and among local jurisdictions. You should hire an experienced local attorney to help you negotiate and document your lease.

"Table for four? Let me check..."

Chapter One

The Basic Restaurant Lease

Our starting point is the lease for a "freestanding" or "stand-alone" restaurant not located in a shopping center or other multi-tenant environment. The provisions of this lease are common to all restaurant leases. In later chapters we will examine modifications of these provisions that are appropriate for restaurants in other settings.

Letter of Intent. Most lease negotiations begin with the parties signing a letter of intent ("LOI") that sets forth the key provisions of the lease. (See Appendix A for a sample LOI.) The LOI includes a description of the premises, the term of the lease (including options to extend the term), the rent, the permitted use, the parties' respective construction obligations, and any other items the parties deem important. The LOI serves as a guideline for preparing the first draft of a lease; it almost always states that it is not binding on the parties. Negotiators approach the LOI from differing points of view, with attitudes ranging from the dismissive ("the LOI is just an invitation to negotiate") to the restrictive ("the LOI is the bible of the negotiation"). The truth lies somewhere in between; the parties should live with their general agreement as reflected in the LOI, but they should expect the deal to evolve as the tenant learns more about the location and the landlord learns more about the proposed restaurant. One advantage of starting with an LOI is that it allows the parties to determine if there is a fundamental disagreement in terms (e.g., the tenant expected to lease the space overlooking the park, but the landlord was offering the space next to the motorcycle repair shop), or an insurmountable impediment to the deal (e.g., the landlord require tenants to remain open seven days a week, but the tenant never operates on Sundays).

Tenant Entities. Most restaurant owners form a limited liability company, corporation or similar protective entity to sign the lease and operate the restaurant. These entities, when properly formed and maintained, can shield an owner's personal assets from creditors of the restaurant in the event of insolvency or bankruptcy, and from lawsuits arising out of personal injury or violations of law. As useful as these entities may be, they are not likely to protect your personal assets from liability to the landlord under your lease. Landlords usually require individual members or shareholders of these entities to become personally liable to the landlord by signing a "guaranty" of the payment of rent and performance of other lease obligations. Signing a guaranty may subject you to substantial liability if the tenant defaults under the lease. This liability may include delinquent rent, the cost to restore the premises to their condition prior to the commencement of the term, some portion of the rent owing after lease termination, the unamortized portion of tenant improvement allowances and rent concessions, and the landlord's legal fees. There are ways to limit your liability under a guaranty. One is to set a maximum dollar amount that the landlord may recover under the guaranty. Another is to ask for a "good guy" guaranty that limits a guarantor's liability to payment of delinquent rent, provided the tenant notifies the landlord of the tenant's inability to continue operating and promptly surrenders the premises in good condition. The "good-guy" guaranty saves the landlord the time and expense of evicting a non-cooperative tenant who may tie up the property for months with legal challenges to the eviction, bankruptcy filings, and other delaying tactics. Most landlords who know a tenant's business is failing would prefer to start looking for a new tenant as soon as possible. It is easier to find a new tenant if the landlord can give some assurance that the existing tenant will surrender the premises without a fight.

Guaranties signed by multiple members or shareholders of a tenant are usually "joint and several," allowing the landlord to collect from any or all guarantors in such amounts as he sees fit. If one investor is relatively wealthy but owns only 1% of the restaurant, then the landlord may collect 100% of the damages from her. That is obviously not a fair result from her point of view. To avoid this outcome, investors who sign a joint and several guaranty should also enter into a "contribution agreement." A contribution agreement provides that, as among themselves, the investors are liable for percentages of amounts actually paid under the guaranty equal to their respective percentage ownership interests in the restaurant. If the wealthy 1% investor pays $100,000 to the landlord to satisfy a judgment under the guaranty, then the contribution agreement will provide that she is liable for only 1% of that amount, or $1,000, and her fellow owners are required to reimburse her the other $99,000. Of course, one or more of the other investors may not have enough money to meet the reimbursement obligation. In such case, the contribution agreement usually provides for some portion of the non-reimbursing owner's interest in the business to be transferred to the investor owed the reimbursement.

Here is an example of why you should shield personal assets from business liabilities.

Term. A restaurant lease typically has an initial term of five to ten years, and includes two or more options for the tenant to extend the term for periods of five years each. The options are important whether or not your restaurant is successful. If your business is a success, then the options will ensure that you have the right to stay in the premises for as long as possible without having to negotiate a new lease. If your business fails, then the options will ensure that there is sufficient time remaining in the lease term to interest potential buyers of your lease. Do not sign a lease that states that the options are "personal" to the original tenant or otherwise provides that the options may not be transferred to a subsequent tenant; this will make it very difficult to find a buyer for your business unless there is substantial time remaining in the initial lease term.

You can ask for as many options as you want, but only the first few option terms are likely have a predetermined rent. Rent for the later option terms will probably be a fair market rent set by arbitration at the time you exercise the option. If you must exercise an option without knowing the rent, then the lease should include a right to rescind the exercise of the option if the rent turns out to be much higher than expected. The landlord may try to convince you that fair market rent options are of little value because, all things being equal, a rational landlord would prefer to keep an existing successful restaurant paying a fair market rent rather than look for another tenant to pay the same rent. This sounds logical, and it might be true if all restaurants were of equal value to landlords. But from the landlord's point of view, a national chain is often preferable to a regional chain or local restaurant on the assumptions that the financial stability of the national chain minimizes the potential for a default and the name recognition of the national chain adds value to the building. You could operate a successful hamburger stand for years, never miss a rent payment, and still the landlord might replace you with a McDonalds paying the same rent. Don't rely on the landlord's verbal assurance that as long as you are doing well you can continue to extend the term. Make the landlord put it in writing.

 Don't Depend Upon the Kindness of Strangers . . . or Landlords.

The owner of a successful restaurant got along well with his landlord. The lease term expired years ago, and the tenant had long-since exercised his last option to extend the term, but the landlord kept extending the lease term (with minimal rent increases) anyway. The tenant spent a fortune renovating his restaurant when he had only a year remaining in the term. He then received a letter from the landlord reminding him that his lease would expire in a year, and that there could be no further extension of the lease term. The tenant learned that the landlord's son had assumed control of the property, and that the son was not as nice as his father. The tenant eventually negotiated an extension, but had to accept a large rent increase.

Rent. Rent will be a big part of your budget, so an understanding of what is included in rent is essential to your planning. Rent may consist of several components, including base rent, percentage rent, amortization of a tenant improvement allowance, and operating expenses.

Base Rent. Nearly all leases have a fixed annual base rent, payable monthly in equal installments. Restaurants typically receive free or reduced rent, or a combination of both, for the first few months of the lease term (but you have to ask!). The expense of opening a restaurant and the time required to build a steady clientele make the first few months particularly challenging from a cash-flow standpoint, and a sophisticated landlord will understand this.

Percentage Rent. In addition to annual base rent, restaurants often pay rent calculated as a percentage of the restaurant's "gross sales" in excess of a specified "breakpoint." The breakpoint is expressed in dollars or by a formula. The definitions of gross sales and breakpoint are subject to negotiation.

"Gross sales" means the total revenue derived from sales of food and beverages to customers. In order to avoid paying percentage rent on unrelated revenue, the gross sales definition should exclude items such as refunds, sales taxes, off-site catering, sales of fixtures and equipment, insurance proceeds, credit card fees, bad debts for house accounts, the value of complimentary meals and meals sold to employees at a discount, charitable contributions, and gift certificates sold but not redeemed.

The breakpoint may be either a "natural breakpoint" (i.e., the amount of gross sales that, when multiplied by the percentage rent rate, equals the annual base rent), or an "artificial breakpoint" agreed upon through negotiation. If your annual base rent is $60,000, and your percentage rent rate is 6%, then the natural breakpoint is $1,000,000 (.06 x $1,000,000 = $60,000). Although the landlord gets no percentage rent on gross sales below the breakpoint, the annual base rent of $60,000 guarantees the landlord the equivalent of 6% of the first $1,000,000 in gross sales. If your annual gross sales exceed $1,000,000, then, in addition to annual base rent, you will pay percentage rent equal to 6% of each dollar of gross sales over $1,000,000. Assuming your annual gross sales are $1,300,000, then you would pay $60,000 in base rent and $18,000 in percentage rent (.06 x $300,000 = $18,000). Percentage rent is calculated on an annual basis, but is often paid monthly commencing in the first calendar month in which gross sales for the calendar year exceed the breakpoint. For partial years, the breakpoint is reduced pro rata based upon the number of days in the year (e.g., if the rent commencement date is February 1, meaning there are 334 days remaining in the calendar year, then the breakpoint for the partial year is equal to the original breakpoint multiplied by 334/365).

Amortization of Tenant Improvement Allowance.   Sometimes the lease includes a separate calculation of the monthly amount necessary to repay a tenant improvement allowance provided by the landlord. The allowance is stated as a separate item to avoid making it subject to the annual increases in base rent that are typical in most leases.

Operating Expenses. Freestanding restaurants are generally leased on a "triple-net" basis, requiring the tenant to assume responsibility for the maintenance and repair of the premises, pay all real estate taxes on the premises, and maintain casualty insurance on the premises.

Maintenance and Repair Costs. Unexpected maintenance and repair costs can result in financial hardship, so before signing your lease, hire a contractor to inspect the building components, including the roof, the heating, ventilating and cooling systems ("HVAC"), and all electrical, plumbing, and fire and life safety systems, to learn their condition and to determine if they are subject to any warranties. It is reasonable to ask the landlord to retain responsibility for repairs to the roof, foundation and other structural elements of the building. If you are required to pay for capital improvements near the end of the term (e.g., replacing the air conditioning compressor), then the cost should be amortized over the useful life of the improvements, and you should pay only that portion of the cost attributable to the remaining lease term.

Taxes. In some jurisdictions, property tax increases are limited by statute. However, taxes may increase substantially upon a sale of the property or other triggering event (such as a long-term lease). Similarly, property taxes may be temporarily reduced on account of a decline in property values, but may increase to prior levels as the real estate market recovers. You should assume that your landlord will sell the building at some point during your lease term and you should budget for any resulting tax increase. You can ask your landlord for protection against these increases, but don't expect a positive response.

Insurance. The lease should specifically identify required insurance coverages and policy limits. If you serve alcohol, then in addition to standard commercial liability insurance, you will be required to carry additional liability coverage (alternatively referred to as liquor liability insurance or dram shop insurance). Watch out for vague statements in the lease requiring you to carry "additional insurance coverage as may be required by landlord from time to time" or to increase policy limits to "amounts typically carried by tenants of similar buildings from time to time." This type of language can result in substantial and unnecessary expense to a tenant.   The landlord will be named as additional insured on all of your insurance policies; your insurance broker will be familiar with the requirements.

Let the Insurance Brokers Earn Their Fees.

Landlords and tenants do not always understand insurance requirements, and many times they over-insure risks or duplicate coverage. The advice of a commercial insurance broker is free, and can save you a great deal of money. Ask your broker to review the insurance provisions of the lease and to coordinate coverage with the landlord's broker.

Due Diligence. You don't need any surprises concerning the condition or allowable use of the property after your lease becomes effective. Although the landlord may have a duty to disclose material defects, you should conduct your own investigation of the property to determine if it is suitable for your use. This process is known as due diligence. Even if your landlord is very forthcoming about the condition of the property, the landlord may not be aware of all defective conditions, and some conditions that are unacceptable to you may not seen as defects by the landlord.

Check the permitted uses of adjacent properties - you might be unpleasantly surprised.

Reports and Studies. You should ask the landlord to provide you with all reports, studies and other materials available regarding the property, including environmental reports, surveys, physical inspection reports, warranties, and equipment manuals and specifications. Your attorney should review a current title report showing restrictions of record affecting the property. Occasionally, restrictions on the sale of alcohol may be present, or other parties may have the right to use the parking areas or driveways in connection with an adjacent business, or the right to maintain billboards or other signage on the property. Parking may prove to be inadequate to meet governmental regulations, or to serve the number of diners required to meet revenue projections

So Why Is This Building Vacant?

Before you commit to a site, you should play detective. Visit the property at different times of the day and become familiar with on-site and off-site conditions. What is the traffic like? Do signals permit cars to easily enter the parking lot? Does the lot flood when it rains? Determine prior uses of the property and investigate why businesses failed there. Read reviews of restaurants that previously occupied the premises and see if the critics disliked more than the food or service ("The new steakhouse on Elm is great, if you don't mind shouting over the rumble of the freight trains that pass by every hour."). Talk to nearby business owners to determine if they are aware of any issues of concern. Bring a few friends with you and ask them if they see anything that might discourage them from patronizing a restaurant at the site. As with any business decision, you must do your homework.

Permits and Licenses. Even if zoning regulations allow a restaurant at your proposed site, you will have to secure a building permit in order to construct your improvements. If your restaurant will offer alcoholic beverages, then you will also need a liquor license. A full set of construction drawings generally must accompany a building permit application, and detailed background information on the restaurant's principals is usually required to be included in a liquor license application. These applications can take substantial time to prepare and may require a lengthy governmental review period followed by revision and resubmission of drawings or applications. In some instances a public hearing may be required. Consider hiring professional consultants to expedite the process, especially if you need any sort of zoning waiver or other special consideration. Many expediters are former employees of the agencies from which you will be seeking permits; they know what goes on behind the scenes, and they have friendships in the agencies that may prove helpful.

Tenant Improvements. Restaurants require more extensive (and expensive) improvements than general retailers, including additional air conditioning and electrical power, filtration and venting equipment, grease traps, and fire-extinguishing systems. Whether performed by the landlord or the tenant, this work is commonly referred to as "tenant improvements." Because the landlord is usually responsible for the basic mechanical, electrical, and plumbing work in the premises, your lease should include a detailed work letter with specifications sufficient to support these above-standard improvements. (See Appendix B for a sample work letter.) An architect or contractor should prepare the work letter.

Which Comes First – Signing the Lease or Due Diligence?

Due diligence is expensive. If you conduct investigations before you sign your lease, then you run the risk that the landlord will lease the property to someone else and you will have wasted your time and money. If you sign your lease before your investigations are complete, then you risk being stuck with property that you cannot use due to problems revealed through due diligence. There is a simple solution to this dilemma: sign the lease first, but include a contingency period during which you may conduct studies and apply for permits and terminate the lease if your investigations reveal unacceptable conditions. Landlords are wary of contingency periods because they allow the tenant to tie-up the property for months and give the tenant an opening to renegotiate lease provisions. Nevertheless, contingency periods are commonly included in restaurant leases. The landlord may also need contingency period, perhaps to secure building permits, or to secure waivers of exclusive use rights or restrictions in other tenants' leases. You should not have to start your due diligence until landlord satisfies its contingencies.

Rent Commencement. Rent commencement should not be tied to a fixed date; the process of securing permits and constructing improvements can be delayed for many reasons beyond the tenant's control. The best solution is to agree to use "reasonable efforts" to complete the tenant improvements and commence business operations as soon as possible, but this open-ended period is not usually acceptable to the landlord. A fair compromise is to establish a timetable for actions required of landlord and tenant, and for each action required of tenant to be performed within a certain number of days following landlord's completion of its action or, if the parties must wait for a governmental agency to inspect work, following such inspection. (See Appendix C for a sample construction timeline.).

Requirements to Open and Operate; Permitted Use. Even though rent may have commenced, a freestanding restaurant should not be required to open for business by a fixed date, or to operate continuously during the lease term after it opens. However, if your lease requires you to pay percentage rent, the landlord may push you to operate seven days a week from early morning to late night so as to maximize gross sales. But gross sales are of no value to the tenant unless they are profitable. The lease should state the minimum hours of operation and specify that during those hours the tenant will operate the restaurant in a manner designed to maximize profitable gross sales.

Unless the lease includes a percentage rent clause, the operator of a freestanding restaurant should be subject to few, if any, restrictions on the use of the premises, aside from a general restriction that the premises shall be used solely for the operation of a restaurant. The landlord should not have any control over the restaurant's menu, theme or décor, and there should be no restrictions on the sale of alcoholic beverages in compliance with applicable laws. The use clause should allow the restaurant to sell hats, shirts and other merchandise bearing the name or logo of the restaurant. If applicable, you may also want to specifically retain the right to use the premises to prepare food for off-site catering. A multi-unit chain restaurant should have the right to operate in the same manner as its other locations in the region in which the premises are located. The use clause should account for changes in consumer preference or evolution of the restaurant's concept; for example, a restaurant that presently serves only fried chicken might someday add grilled or barbecued chicken or offer a chicken salad or sandwich. If you do agree to limit your use to a particular style or concept, then the lease should require the landlord to reasonably approve a change in that style or concept upon your written request. If the use is limited to a specific style or concept, then it will be difficult to assign the lease or to sell the restaurant without a right to make a change.

Parking. In most jurisdictions, zoning ordinances require restaurants to maintain more parking spaces per square foot of building floor area than general retailers. If your building was previously used as a restaurant, then parking may be adequate. But if the building's last use was general retail, then you may find that the premises have a serious parking shortage. Parking is sometimes available in nearby garages or surface lots, but this will require an agreement with a third party that may be costly and time-consuming to negotiate and document. Off-site parking agreements often require approval of the local zoning authority, a requirement that will add more delay to the process. If you plan to provide valet parking, make sure it is permitted by local ordinances. If customer parking will be provided in off-site garages or lots, you will need to arrange for a validation system. Finally, even if your building was last used as a restaurant, parking requirements may have changed, and your application for a building permit may result in imposition of the new requirements on your site.

Security Interest in Fixtures and Equipment. The lease or applicable law may grant your landlord a security interest in your fixtures and equipment. This allows the landlord to sell your fixtures and equipment if the lease is terminated due to your default. If you plan to lease or finance any equipment or fixtures, the lease should require the landlord to sign an agreement granting the financing company a security interest in the leased or financed items superior to the landlord's security interest. This agreement will also grant the financing company a right to enter upon onto the property and remove financed equipment and fixtures.

<u>Licenses and Easements for Off-Site Parking.</u>

Off-site parking may be secured by license or easement.

A license is a contractual right that may be revoked pursuant to its terms and that is generally personal to the original recipient of the license. Parking rights created by a license do not automatically transfer to the new owner of the restaurant upon an assignment of the lease or sublease of the premises.

An easement is an interest in real property for a period of time. It cannot be revoked (absent some default under the easement agreement), and it "runs with the land," meaning it is not personal to the original recipient of the easement, but belongs to all subsequent owners of the property and their tenants.

Whether you need a license or an easement is often the determination of local zoning authorities. In most states, a license agreement can be drafted to provide protections reasonably similar to an easement. Just make sure whatever agreement you use cannot be revoked without good cause and can be transferred to any buyer of the restaurant.

<u>Default</u>. Be wary of any rights the landlord may have to terminate the lease upon your default. These rights may result in a forfeiture of your investment. You should not be deemed to be in default under the lease until you have received written notice of the alleged breach of the lease and have been given adequate time to correct the problem. Don't accept a cure period of a particular number of days for a non-monetary default (i.e., a default other than your failure to pay rent) that cannot be cured quickly or easily. The lease may provide that you will commence the cure of a non-monetary default within a specified period of time, but the cure period for a non-monetary default should be open-ended as long as you are diligently prosecuting the cure.

<u>Exit Strategies; Assignment and Subleasing</u>. If your restaurant is not successful, then you will need to close with a minimum of financial pain. One of your most valuable rights is the ability to assign your lease to another restaurant. This is often the only way to recover the cost of tenant improvements, including permanent fixtures such as cooking systems and walk-in coolers. Even if your lease allows it, the cost of removing improvements and fixtures, and restoring the premises, is generally prohibitive. The landlord may insist on receiving all or a portion of any payment you receive for an assignment, after deducting your unamortized improvement costs and any transaction costs; try to get the landlord to agree to take no more than fifty percent. The landlord's conditions for approving an assignment should be specifically described in the lease. For a freestanding restaurant, conditions should be limited to the assignee's ability to perform financial and operating covenants of the lease.

 Assignment. Sublease. What's the Difference?

Assignment and sublease are terms that are used to describe some form of a transfer of the right to occupy the premises.

An assignment transfers the lease to a new tenant (assignee), and the assignee assumes the duty to pay rent and perform all other obligations under the lease. The assignee becomes directly liable to the landlord under the lease. The original tenant is not released from liability (unless he gets very lucky!), but the assignee is primarily liable for all lease obligations. The original tenant is not responsible for a lease default unless the assignee is unable to cure it and has insufficient assets to satisfy a judgment.

A sublease gives a new tenant (subtenant) the right to occupy the premises, but the original tenant remains liable for the payment of rent and the performance of all other obligations under the lease. The landlord has no lease or other contract with the subtenant and can evict the subtenant if the original tenant fails to pay rent or perform other obligations. The subtenant's protection is to secure an agreement (a "recognition agreement" or "nondisturbance agreement") from the landlord allowing the subtenant to remain in the premises after a default so long as the subtenant cures any defaults and agrees to pay the rent and perform all other lease obligations for the remainder of the term.

Perhaps business will improve soon…

Chapter Two

Restaurants in Shopping Centers

In this chapter we consider leases for restaurants in shopping centers. A "shopping center" is any multi-tenant retail complex under common ownership or control, from a neighborhood strip center to a regional mall. One of the defining characteristics of a shopping center is the presence of common areas not reserved for any particular tenant, including parking areas and walkways, and, in larger centers, food courts, children's play areas, and restrooms. Mixed-use projects and hotels, both of which are unique multi-tenant environments that blend retail and non-retail uses, are examined in later chapters.

<u>Parking</u>. Restaurants require two to three times more parking spaces than general retail businesses. Most shopping center leases do not provide meaningful parking protections for the restaurant tenant, either in terms of the number of spaces or their location. The lease should require the landlord to maintain a specified number of conveniently located parking spaces for use by your customers. This is an area where you may have to dig in your heels; landlords don't like to give up control of their parking areas, especially to smaller tenants. Landlords view parking fields as areas of future development, and no leasing manager wants to have to tell the landlord that they can't build a new movie theater because Mom and Pop's Sandwich Shop controls the area where the theater is to be located!

If you look at an aerial view of a typical shopping center, the sea of parking spaces surrounding the buildings would appear to be sufficient to accommodate the requirements of any restaurant. But the only parking spaces that are of true value to a restaurant tenant are those spaces located near the restaurant and available to its patrons. Before you start negotiating your lease, decide which parking spaces are essential to your operation. Ask the landlord to specifically identify these spaces in the lease and to agree not to reduce their number or change their location. If you provide take-out service, it is helpful to have a few parking spaces reserved for customers picking up orders. If parking is provided in a multi-level structure, directional signage should be installed to guide customers to the most convenient parking area. Access to the structure from adjacent public streets, and from the structure to the restaurant, should be provided at all times when you are open for business. If the landlord charges for parking, then you may want to negotiate the right for your customers to park free or at a reduced fee under a validation system. This system should be negotiated in the lease and not left to some future parking management agreement or plan. Your chef and manager should have reserved spaces near the restaurant so that they can come and go during the day without worrying about finding parking.

Carefully consider the effect of provisions that allow parking areas to be closed for street fairs, farmers markets and other special events, or that allow the landlord to sell parking to patrons of nearby stadiums, arenas, theaters, convention centers and similar venues. Even if your lease provides for protected parking, the closure of other shopping center parking areas may result in other stores' patrons parking in your protected area.

The farmers market might be a good idea, in moderation . . .

A related concern involves the growing presence of mobile food trucks in shopping centers and on adjacent streets. Many tenants resent these traveling food vendors because they don't pay rent or contribute to the upkeep of the shopping center. Should you allow them near your restaurant? Some tenants believe the foot traffic that food trucks bring to the shopping center will expose their restaurant to potential new patrons, while others see the trucks as unwanted competition.

Signage. You will have a lot of competition at a shopping center, so you should have the right to maintain advertising and directional signage at various locations. Your lease should provide for signs to be placed in all parking areas and other common of areas directing customers to your restaurant. You should be treated at least as favorably as any other similarly sized restaurant at the shopping center with respect to the number, size, and location of directional signs. You should be included on all mall directories, as well as in any print or electronic advertising in which any other restaurant is included. The entire front of your premises should be reserved for your signage only.

Access. Common areas inside shopping centers that once were open and uncluttered have been engulfed by a rising tide of cell phone kiosks, candy carts, teeth whitening booths, massage chairs and anything else the landlord can think of to generate an extra dollar of rent. This is not a big problem provided the clutter does not prevent customers from reaching your restaurant before you close for the evening. The lease should identify the main access to the restaurant for both pedestrians and vehicles from all parking and other common areas, including key escalators and elevators, and the landlord should not be permitted to obstruct, relocate, or close these access routes. The landlord should also be required to repair any mechanical failures of escalators or elevators immediately. Access should remain available during all hours of your operation.

Visibility. The landlord should not allow kiosks, carts, booths, ATM's or other items or structures to obstruct the view of your restaurant from the common areas. These types of remote merchandising units are a fact of life, but the landlord should agree to a zone around your restaurant's windows and doors that will be free from obstruction. The landlord should not allow any buildings to be constructed that would obstruct visibility; this generally requires a site plan that is marked to show an area of unobstructed visibility from your restaurant to the common areas, as well as height restrictions on buildings that can be located in the common areas.

Remodeling. The shopping center will be remodeled occasionally, and you may suffer some loss of business during the renovation period. The lease should protect access and visibility during remodeling to the extent reasonably possible. Construction barricades and detours can make businesses invisible or inaccessible to all but the most loyal customers. The landlord will usually offer a rent reduction for the inconvenience caused by construction. However, you should consider asking to be reimbursed for lost sales, which may be substantially greater than the amount of the rent. The problem with the lost sales remedy is that it is difficult to prove that a decline in sales results solely from the remodeling.

Free Advertising.

When remodeling occurs in the shopping center, ask your landlord to apply graphics bearing your restaurant's logo to some of the construction barricades. This will help your customers find you during construction, and it's free advertising.

Permitted Use. The permitted-use clause determines the allowable scope of a tenant's use of the premises, including the concept, style and, in some cases, menu, of the restaurant. The landlord wants to restrict each tenant to as narrow a use as possible in order to allow maximum flexibility in attracting other restaurants. By limiting the permitted use of each restaurant, the landlord is able to attract a diverse group of tenants and create a tenant mix that is beneficial to all. Often the landlord will suggest attaching a menu to the lease that lists everything that you may sell. This is too restrictive. The landlord should be satisfied with a description of the style and concept of the restaurant.

If the landlord insists on attaching a menu, then you can agree to generally serve the types of items shown on the menu, but retain the right to alter the menu consistent with the style and concept of the restaurant described in the lease.

Covenant to Operate. Most shopping center leases require a restaurant to be open for lunch and dinner every day. Your lease should include the right to close on holidays and for private parties. You should have the right to close for remodeling for a reasonable length of time, or when required by the health department or other local authority, or to complete repairs following casualty.

Exclusive Use Rights. Most shopping center restaurants enjoy exclusive use rights, and at the same time are subject to exclusive use rights granted to other tenants. For example, the lease for a Chinese restaurant may prohibit any other tenant from serving Chinese food. In return for this protection, the operator of the Chinese restaurant may be required to agree not sell food items exclusively reserved to other restaurants. These rights give tenants the opportunity to maximize sales (and the landlord's percentage rent from such sales) by being the only choice for diners who want a particular style of food. You should ask for an exclusive for your style of restaurant that is as broad as possible, and carefully review all exclusive use rights reserved to other tenants to confirm that they will not adversely impact your operation. The other tenants' exclusive use rights should be described in detail on a list attached to your lease. Attach the exact exclusivity language from the other tenants' leases; summaries may be inaccurate. Exclusive use clauses are often surprisingly broad; a fast-food chain that sells only fried chicken may have the exclusive right to sell "prepared chicken." Hopefully, your landlord will have negotiated appropriate exceptions to these restrictions (e.g., the chicken exclusive should not apply to full-service restaurants, or to chicken used as a component of another dish such as sweet and sour chicken in a Chinese restaurant or chicken lasagna in an Italian restaurant), but nothing should be assumed. Most restaurants are vigilant when it comes to protecting their exclusive rights, so if an existing exclusive in favor of another tenant will impact your operation, then ask the landlord to request that the other tenant modify or waive their exclusive for your benefit.

 Use the Letter of Intent to Protect Your Exclusive Use.

In a new shopping center, the landlord is often negotiating with many tenants at one time. If your negotiations drag on, some of the exclusive use rights you thought you would get may be given to other tenants. In a multi-tenant setting, the letter of intent should be used to put the landlord on notice of your required exclusive use rights. After the letter of intent is signed, the landlord should not give any other tenant the right to use its premises in a manner that would violate your exclusive. Because letters of intent are usually non-binding, this rule is not always followed, and the issues of exclusives and exceptions are often revisited a number of times as negotiations progress. In any case, it's worth a try!

Co-Tenancy. There is no denying the synergy created by a diverse group of restaurants located near each other. There is also no denying the disaster that awaits a restaurant that opens by itself with construction barricades around it, or whose neighboring restaurants begin to close and are not replaced. To ensure that you benefit from this synergy rather than face disaster, your lease should require that certain restaurants be open for business at the time you commence operations, and that certain restaurants remain open during the term of your lease. Co-tenants are usually identified by style of cuisine, floor area, and location. The typical remedy for a co-tenancy failure is a rent abatement or reduction for some period of time, at the end of which period the tenant has the option to resume paying full rent or, if the co-tenancy failure is continuing, to terminate the lease. The landlord often wants the tenant to demonstrate a loss of sales due to the co-tenancy failure before becoming entitled to a rent reduction. This sounds reasonable, but it is not. Numerous variables may contribute to a decline in sales, including unseasonable weather, general economic downturn, change in consumer taste, and closure of other stores at the shopping center. It is probably impossible to tell what portion of lost sales are attributable to a co-tenancy failure as opposed to the other factors. One compromise is for the tenant to pay only percentage rent, with the breakpoint being tenant's operating costs. For example, if it costs a restaurant $50,000 per month to operate, then the tenant would pay percentage rent on all sales above $50,000 per month for so long as the co-tenancy failure continued.

Relocation. A relocation clause gives a landlord the right to move a tenant to a different location in the shopping center, usually in connection with remodeling or expansion of the project. Relocation does not occur often, and when it does, the landlord usually acts in good faith. However, you should assume that your landlord will use the relocation clause to move you to a dark corner of the shopping center and put his brother-in-law's restaurant in your old space. Don't consent to relocation unless the landlord demonstrates a legitimate need for it. The landlord should deliver written notice of a proposed relocation describing the reason for the relocation, the identities of other tenants being relocated, and floor area, configuration and location of the new premises. The new location should be exposed to similar pedestrian traffic as the old one, and should have similar types of businesses around it. The landlord should pay all costs to construct a similar restaurant in the new location, as well as all other expenses of relocation. The seating area should be at least as large as in the old premises. If the floor area of the new space larger than the original space, then you should not have to pay rent on the additional floor area.

Radius Restriction. If you are paying percentage rent, then your lease will likely include a radius restriction prohibiting you from operating another restaurant within a specified area. The restriction should apply only to "competing" restaurants (i.e., restaurants whose operations are likely to attract customers who might have otherwise dined at the original restaurant). The landlord's idea of "competition" is often overly broad; your lease should not prohibit you from operating or owning an interest in "any other restaurant." This may be appropriate where a restaurant operator is so well known that customers will follow him anywhere, but generally another restaurant is not truly "competitive" unless it is operated under the same name, serves the same type of cuisine, or has a similar "look and feel." You should not be prohibited from owning a passive interest in another restaurant; you don't want to inadvertently violate the radius restriction by buying a mutual fund that holds shares of McDonalds. If you violate the radius restriction, then the preferred remedy is to include sales from the competing location in the gross sales of the leased premises for purposes of calculating percentage rent.

 Site Plans: What You See Is Not Always What You Get.

The tenant's rights under the lease should apply to the entire shopping center. But what is the "shopping center?" Don't assume that the "shopping center" that is defined in the lease is the same as what you see on the ground. Watch out for definitions and drawings that omit portions of the land and improvements that appear to be part of the shopping center. Landlords often divide projects into zones, and only the particular zone in which your restaurant is located may be included in the definition of "shopping center." In such a case, your exclusive use may apply to only one wing of the mall because that is all that is identified as the "shopping center" on the site plan. It is essential that a detailed site plan be attached to the lease identifying all the property included in the "shopping center," including areas that may be developed in the future. The lease may identify certain premises that are not subject to the landlord's control, such as a major department store; however, you should insist that such premises be included in the definition of "shopping center" if and when the landlord gains control of such an area.

Common Area Maintenance Costs. Shopping center tenants pay a portion of the costs of operating, insuring, maintaining, and repairing the parking areas, sidewalks, signs, utilities, landscaping and other common areas (common area maintenance costs or CAM). In a gross lease, these charges are included in the rent. In a net lease, the charges are in addition to the base rent. Some leases include just a broad definition of CAM like the one set forth in the first sentence of this paragraph. Other leases devote endless space to listing each component of CAM, and also include a statement that other items not listed may be included. In either case, it is important that you exclude items that are not properly your responsibility (See Appendix D for a sample list of common CAM exclusions.), and that you insist upon receiving the right to perform annual audits of CAM expenses. You should try to negotiate a maximum annual increase in the CAM expenses for which you are charged, although the landlord will want to exclude costs of insurance, taxes, and other items outside its control.

 Looking for Your CAM Statement? Try the Fiction Section.

It is pointless to negotiate a maximum annual CAM increase, or to negotiate CAM exclusions, if you don't carefully review the annual statements of CAM expenses provided by your landlord. Landlords sometimes "forget" that you have a maximum increase or specific CAM exclusions, and charge you more than you are obligated to pay under your lease. Sometimes the landlord's "forgetfulness" is due to the landlord having many leases with different CAM provisions and not wanting to spend the time and money to review each lease and tailor each tenant's CAM billings to those individual leases. Instead, landlord sends out the same statement to all the tenants and relies on each tenant to notify it of any mistake. This problem is compounded if the same errors are repeated on each annual statement and can add up to thousands of dollars over your lease term.

Utilities and Trash. The landlord may provide submeters to measure your consumption of water, gas and electricity. If not, then allocation of the costs of these utilities should be made based upon the floor areas of the various businesses sharing the utilities. Restaurants are heavy users of these utilities, so it is the other retailers who are generally worried about the allocation; to make an equitable allocation, the landlord may create separate cost pools for restaurants and other retailers, assigning a greater share of costs to the restaurants due to their heavier use.

The landlord will usually provide shared trash facilities. You should make sure they are adequate for your needs and located far enough from your restaurant that they can't be smelled, yet close enough that your employees don't have to pack an overnight bag to take out the trash. Restaurants produce more trash than other retailers, so landlords may create separate cost pools for restaurants, requiring them to bear a higher respective percentage of trash costs than the retailers. You may also encounter a trash compactor system that is accessed with key cards or codes unique to each tenant and which measures the weight and/or volume of trash added by each tenant. In warm climates, trash may be stored in refrigerated rooms to minimize odor.

Delivery Issues. Restaurants in shopping centers may be required to share loading docks and delivery areas with other restaurants and retailers. The tenants sharing the loading docks should not be allowed to leave their trucks at the dock longer than necessary to load or unload them; some retailers are in the habit of keeping their trucks in the loading dock for hours at a time while they leisurely unload them and the driver takes his afternoon break. In general, restaurant deliveries should be given priority as they are usually small and can be unloaded quickly. Restrictions on hours of deliveries should be carefully reviewed; these restrictions may prove particularly problematic for restaurants receiving perishable foods such as fish or produce from a supplier distributing to multiple customers. The restrictions should not apply to FedEx, UPS or other carriers whose delivery times are beyond tenant's control. Leases may restrict receiving deliveries through the front door, but this may be a standard lease provision that does not fit the particular project for which it is being used. The tenant should review the receiving areas and their proximity to the restaurant to make certain that they are adequate; if not, the tenant should retain the option to accept deliveries through the front door.

Know when deliveries are arriving and make sure there is space for the truck.

Chapter Three

Restaurants in Mixed-Use Projects

Mixed-use projects, incorporating retail stores, restaurants, offices, and residences, provide the opportunity to live, work, shop and dine in a single location. Although it is convenient to have customers living and working an elevator ride away, it is a challenge to maintain harmony among the various groups that share the project. An additional complication may arise from the fact that different parties may own the various components of the project. When a dispute arises, it is essential to have a lease that anticipates and addresses the problem. Most lease forms do not fit well with mixed-use projects, and this chapter will address some of the most overlooked issues.

 Wow, Look at All These Documents!

The lease is not the only document that governs the operation of a restaurant in a mixed-use project. There is generally an agreement among the owners of the project's components called a Declaration of Covenants, Conditions and Restrictions or something similar. This declaration governs the use of the project by the various occupants. Even though you will not sign the declaration, you will be bound by many of its terms that are "incorporated by reference" into your lease. Think of it as "invisible" ink – you can't see the provisions, but they are there! To actually "see" the "incorporated provisions" you need the other document where they are written with "visible" ink. To further complicate matters, if there are different owners of the office space and the retail space, then there may be a second, commercial declaration that governs the use of these two areas. For example, the overall declaration may divide the parking between residential users and commercial users, and the commercial declaration may further divide the commercial parking areas between retail and office uses. These documents may seem daunting, but it is important that you review and understand them. Your lease will probably allow your landlord to amend and modify the declarations in the future; if so, you should require the landlord to give you advance notice of proposed changes so you have time to raise any objections. Unless applicable law or your lease provides otherwise, you should not be bound by any amendment to the extent that is in conflict with your lease.

Noise and Odor. Noise and cooking odor are a natural part of the restaurant experience, enjoyed (at best) or tolerated (at worst) by the diner during the meal, but quickly forgotten upon leaving the restaurant. But since residents and workers in a mixed-use project are already at home or work, they have to live with the noise and odor at all times. The smell of cinnamon rolls baking in the oven and the clinking of spoons in coffee cups may encourage locals to visit in the morning, but by evening the odor of sizzling fish and the honking of car horns by parking attendants may push tired residents and workers to the breaking point. The patronage and support of these residents and workers will be crucial to your restaurant's success, so the issue of noise and odor control requires thoughtful consideration. Your lease should also specify the location of the trash storage and compaction areas. Kitchen exhaust should be vented away from the residences and offices.

Noise, whether generated inside or outside a restaurant, is a big concern for the restaurant operator. Inside noise can be contained by adequate sound insulation. The type and rating of the insulation, and responsibility for its cost, should be specified in your lease. Controlling noise from patio and other outside areas is a more difficult problem. There is often a local curfew, but if not, you and the landlord will have to agree on a reasonable time for the patio noise to cease. Don't be so focused on containing noise and odor within the restaurant that you forget to protect your restaurant against noise and odor from those around, above and below you. Of special concern are movie theaters, bowling alleys, and health clubs, which generate substantial vibrations.

 The Landlord's Money-Saving Plan Stinks.

Venting at the rooftop is critical if you are cooking odorous foods. I once represented a tenant opening a seafood restaurant in a new thirty-floor mixed-use project. The city was allowing odors to be vented at the tenth floor, saving the landlord the expense of running a duct up the entire building. The tenant insisted on venting to the roof. He explained his primary source of business was the residents of the tower and he did not want to subject them to offensive cooking odors. The landlord agreed, despite the extra expense. This shows the importance of the tenant being involved in the lease negotiations. It is doubtful that anyone not experienced in the day-to-day operation of a restaurant would recognize the problem created by venting at a lower floor.

Parking. The parking issues in mixed-use projects are complex due to the varying needs and expectations of retail and restaurant customers and employees, office workers and visitors, and residents and their guests. Many of these projects have a single valet-parking service for all the commercial businesses, so make sure there is adequate signage directing patrons to your restaurant. During nights and weekends, patrons should also have access to office parking spaces. Guests of residents should not be permitted to park in retail spaces, and that there is some enforcement of this restriction by project security personnel. Make sure your employees understand and follow the parking rules.

Marketing. Office workers and residents represent a main source of repeat business for restaurants in a mixed-use project, but it may be difficult to market to these potential customers because rules often prohibit distribution of flyers, coupons and other advertising media within the complex. More acceptable methods of building a customer base may include sponsoring social gatherings within the project, offering incentives to customers who refer other staff or residents of the building, providing delivery and catering services within the project, and being included on any project directories, signs, electronic displays or other multi-tenant advertising media.

Phased Construction. The retail floors of a mixed-use project are often completed before the office and residential floors. If the exterior of the building is complete, the garage is finished and accessible, and there are no impediments to customers' use of common areas, then the construction of interior tenant improvements is unlikely to disrupt restaurant operations. However, to the extent you are counting on the patronage of residents and office workers in order to meet sales goals, it may be prudent to delay rent commencement until occupancy rates have reached specified levels. If you must open before the project is completed, then "staging" areas for storing equipment and materials and for performing finish work should be confined to areas shown on a site plan attached to your lease. Any construction immediately above, below or adjacent to a retail tenant that creates noise, dust, vibration or odors should be performed outside of your business hours.

Signs. A mixed-use project is large enough to allow many signs to be placed around the exterior of the building, including: blade signs outside each shop; large signs on the facades identifying anchor tenants; landlord's signs offering office and residential space for lease; and, if permitted by local regulations, video screens and electronic billboards capable of displaying multiple advertisements. This menagerie of signage may create "sign clutter" that is confusing or distracting. Your lease should identify a "signage free" area on the building façade around your premises to protect the visibility of your signage. If the project has billboards or video screens used for third-party ads, you should have the right to be represented on such signs, and your landlord should not be allowed to display ads of your competitors.

Common Area Maintenance Costs. Allocating CAM expenses in a mixed-use project is a big challenge for a landlord. Determining if the allocation is reasonable is a bigger challenge for a tenant. The project declaration will provide for CAM expenses to be allocated among the retail, office, and residential users pursuant to a negotiated formula. The CAM expenses allocated to the retail component will be further allocated between the retail stores and restaurants. Given the landlord's discretion to make these allocations, the tenant should have the right to perform annual audits of landlord's books and records as they relate to CAM expenses for the entire project. The landlord may attempt to limit the audit to expenses concerning the retail component, but a determination of the appropriateness of the retail allocation cannot be made without understanding the project allocation. Because retail and restaurant tenants generally pay a straight pass-through of CAM expenses (whereas office tenants pay only increases over a base year, and apartment tenants pay a gross rent with no payment of CAM expenses), landlords have an incentive to place as much of the CAM expense as possible onto the retail component. To the extent parking garage and structure maintenance costs and expenses are included in CAM expenses, all parking fees collected by landlord should be applied against parking garage and structure operating, repair and maintenance costs, with only the balance of unrecovered costs included in CAM expenses.

Patio Area. If the patio is exclusively reserved for your restaurant, then you will generally pay for all tables, chairs, trash containers and other furniture and fixtures to be used on the patio, and you will bus tables, provide trash containers and keep the patio in a clean, orderly and sanitary condition. Depending on your location, access to a patio area may be a year-round or only a seasonal concern. If the patio area is shared among a number of tenants, the landlord should provide security and attendants to maintain the patio in an attractive and usable condition for all tenants, with the costs included in CAM expenses. However, in a smaller center the task is often left to the tenants.

When you clean the patio, be certain to extinguish all open fires.

Chapter Four

Restaurants in Hotels

Nowhere is the landlord more concerned with the day-to-day operation of a restaurant than in a hotel. A hotel may have a difficult time booking meetings or conventions if the reputation of its restaurants declines. Similarly, the restaurant owner must carefully consider the business outlook for the hotel. If a hotel fails to maintain a high occupancy rate or to attract parties and special events, then its restaurants may not attract enough customers to operate profitably. Hotel properties are often owned by investors who lease them to hotel chains. When we speak of the landlord we are referring to a hotel operator and not the property owner. In such cases, the restaurant is a subtenant whose occupancy rights may be subject to termination if the hotel operator loses its lease. (For this reason alone you should not negotiate a lease in a hotel without the assistance of an attorney.)

Ratings. A common standard for measuring the performance of a hotel or restaurant is a rating from a consumer organization (e.g., the AAA Diamond classification). The lease will require the tenant to operate its restaurant in a manner consistent with the hotel's rating level. This is reasonable; but the hotel should agree to maintain such rating throughout the lease term. While ratings are helpful indicators, they are often outdated due to delays in publication. Problems noted in a review may have been corrected before publication, and problems arising following a review may not be noted until months later. Other methods of measuring performance include customer comment cards, surveys, sales data, reviews by professional critics, and anecdotal evidence shared by customers on social-media sites. Because these are all subjective measures of performance, the parties should view them as warning signs of a potential problem. If the problem continues, then ultimately the continued poor performance by one party may allow the other to terminate the lease; however, before that occurs, detailed written notice of the claimed breach should be given and the parties should discuss the issues of concern and work together to solve any problems. After some reasonable period, the parties may enter into a non-binding mediation proceeding. Given the substantial investment of each party and the possible damage to their reputations, a lease termination should be the last resort.

Associations. Restaurants are often operated or associated with talented chefs, successful athletes, popular entertainers, and other celebrities. Your lease may require the continuation of that association, including the use of the celebrity's name. If a hotel expects a celebrity to actively participate in a restaurant's operations, then the level and frequency of such participation (e.g., design of restaurant, menu planning, on-site cooking, meeting and greeting guests, book signings and other special events) should be set forth in your lease. If it is important to you that the hotel remain operating under the flag of a chain known for a high level of service or quality, or that appeals to a particular demographic, then continued operation under that specific flag (or the flag of a comparable chain) should be required in your lease.

Menu. It is reasonable for a hotel to require that you offer a menu broad enough to serve the diverse tastes of its guests. If there are a number of restaurants in the hotel, then the landlord is more likely to allow you to control your menu. When there are multiple restaurants, a landlord is more concerned with ensuring that menu items are not duplicated by its other restaurants. If you operate other restaurants outside the hotel, the landlord may require you to offer similar menus as those restaurants.

You may be required to offer a broad menu if you are operating in a hotel.

Hours of Operation. In general, the hotel will require you to be open for lunch and dinner every day of the year. If you are the only restaurant in the hotel, you will probably be required to open for breakfast. You can expect to be required to operate on all holidays. In order to make certain the restaurant remains available to hotel guests, the portion of the restaurant that you may reserve for private parties may be restricted.

Catering. If you are expected to cater events in hotel facilities, or if you desire to cater events outside the hotel, then the details are usually set forth in a separate agreement. Catering agreements are beyond the scope of this book, but issues to consider include any fee you must pay the hotel for using the kitchen facilities to cater non-hotel functions, the menu and price points that you will be required to offer for on-site functions, and division of labor between the hotel staff and restaurant staff.

Room Service. In most hotels, you will be expected to provide high-quality room service. Depending upon the size or location of the hotel, you may be obligated to provide full-menu room service 24 hours a day, or full-menu room service part of the day and a more limited menu for the remainder of the day. The hotel will want to approve both the full-service and limited-service menus, including the items offered and the prices charged.

Although you will prepare the food, the hotel should provide personnel to take and deliver room-service orders, as well as to retrieve dishes, silverware and trays. Because of the potential liability involved, entry into guest rooms should always be left to hotel staff. The cost of the hotel personnel is often charged back to the restaurant. The restaurant's obligations may include planning and ordering the items to be included in mini-bars.

Guest Signing Privileges. Hotel restaurants are typically obligated to allow guests to charge meals to their rooms. But how do you know that the diner making the charge is actually a guest occupying the room number written on the charge slip? And how do you know that the diner will pay this charge at checkout? There are several methods of identifying legitimate hotel guests, including identification cards that can be read by your point-of-sale system. Your lease should require the hotel to verify the diner's signing privileges and credit limits upon request. Having given such verification, the hotel should be liable for any uncollectible amounts. Verification can be done instantaneously through your link to the hotel's computer network. If that is not an option, then you can use the old-fashioned method of a phone call to the front desk. In either case, the risk of nonpayment is shifted to the hotel. If a guest is planning to charge an unusually large amount, such as for a private party, then the restaurant should be certain to clear that amount (including the gratuity) with the hotel in advance of the event.

The hotel should give you a weekly report reconciling the prior week's room charge activity, accompanied by payment for the charges. If a guest pays his or her hotel charges with a credit card, then the processing fee charged by the card issuer or processor may be deducted from the amount due. The hotel may also impose its own processing fee, but it should not exceed 1% of the charges processed.

Upon checking out of the hotel, a guest may dispute a charge made at your restaurant. The guest may claim not to have made the charge, or may claim that the charge should be reduced or eliminated due to poor service or bad food. If the hotel manager cannot settle the dispute immediately, the hotel may deduct the charge, but reserve the right to collect from the customer following investigation. Your landlord has a legitimate interest in avoiding embarrassment to the hotel and retaining the goodwill of its customers. The lease should provide that the hotel and the restaurant will work together to resolve such disputes.

Alcoholic Beverages. Your restaurant may act as a substitute for a traditional hotel bar, and the availability of alcoholic beverages is important to the landlord. In many jurisdictions, the hotel may hold a master license for the sale of alcoholic beverages, and all restaurants in the hotel will operate under that permit. For these reasons, hotels are very concerned with making sure that restaurants follow all of the rules and restrictions associated with the permit, and will require restaurants to abide by the hotel's standards pertaining to the service of alcoholic beverages. The hotel may require that employees serving alcoholic beverages and their supervisors complete a training program to ensure compliance with all applicable laws and regulations.

 Look for a Successful Restaurant and Hire Its Employees

If you are opening a restaurant in a hotel and will be serving alcohol, consider hiring personnel who have prior experience in hotel restaurants. This is especially helpful when it comes to managers and their assistants. They will be familiar with the complex rules and regulations that govern the service of alcoholic beverages and will help ensure a smooth opening and trouble-free operation.

Staff and Supplies. Your lease will require you to maintain an adequate staff of employees and stock of food, beverages, merchandise and supplies in order to fully meet the demands and requirements of diners. This is a reasonable requirement and assures the hotel that you are prepared to meet whatever demand may exist. However, you should not allow the landlord to interfere in your personnel matters or dictate the specific details of your day-to-day purchases. For example, while the hotel may require that you have a fresh seafood entrée, you should have the sole discretion to determine each day's menu. Also, the hotel may dictate that a range of qualities and prices of wine be offered at your restaurant, but they should not determine which labels and vintages are carried.

Discounted and Complimentary Meals. You may be required to provide complimentary food and beverages ("comps") for certain hotel guests. The landlord will reimburse you the menu price of the comped meal, applicable sales taxes, and a gratuity.

A dispute may arise over the amount the landlord will reimburse for comped wines. Fine wines are an important profit center for any restaurant. The profit has two components: the increase in the value of the wine over time due to its critical acclaim and growing scarcity; and any additional mark-up over the market value that the restaurant is able to charge. If the wine is still available for purchase from the restaurant's distributor, then the reimbursement should be limited to the actual cost to the restaurant to purchase a replacement bottle. If the wine is no longer available, then the landlord should reimburse at least the market value, but whether the landlord should also reimburse any or all of the mark-up is a matter for negotiation.

You may also be required to provide discounted meals to hotel employees while they are on duty. In addition, the hotel's key personnel may be entitled to a discount on food and beverages, including alcoholic beverages. You and the landlord will need to agree upon the percentage discount or the fixed price of the meals, and to a monthly dollar limit on such discounted food and beverages.

Negotiate a limit on the number of hotel employees the restaurant is required to feed.

Promotional Materials, Signage, and In-Room Advertising. Hotel rooms and common areas provide multiple opportunities for promotion. In-room materials may include television channels, guidebooks and informational binders, and tabletop and desktop displays. Outside the room, opportunities include check-in materials, dining guides, phone "on-hold" messaging, signage in elevators, hallways and lobbies, web sites, print advertisements, and off-site advertising (including billboards at airports and along highways). You should have the right to advertise in all these areas to the same extent as other restaurants in the hotel.

Sponsorships. Your landlord may enter into sponsorship or marketing agreements with third parties requiring that only certain products or brands be offered for sale or use within the hotel. For example, there may be an "official coffee" required to be the only coffee served by all restaurants in the hotel. You will be required to abide by such agreements. Whether these agreements would survive an antitrust challenge is an open question, but you are not in a very good position to complain about the arrangement once you have agreed to it in writing by signing your lease.

This crowd may be a little rough for modern gaming authorities.

Gaming Properties. Hotels that include casino operations are subject to strict licensing regulations that will impact your restaurant operation. If your lease is for a new hotel, then the landlord may conduct leasing activities at the same time it seeks its gaming licenses. You may wish to make your lease contingent upon receipt of such licenses. You and your key employees may be required to complete background checks and submit personal and financial information to gaming authorities in order to assist the landlord in receiving its licenses. A lease in a gaming property often mandates strict standards of behavior. Default may be triggered if it is determined that the tenant's presence in the premises has resulted in any of the following: public demonstrations; increased security risks; inconvenience to landlord's patrons or other occupants; interference with the operation or management of the premises; or any complaint lodged against landlord by any regulatory authority.

Chapter Five

Drive-Thru Restaurants

Most of us give little thought to the drive-thru lane at the local quick-serve restaurant. The entire process of studying the menu board, placing an order through the speaker system, and paying and collecting the food through the little window, is such a common ritual of modern life that it might surprise the average person just how much effort goes into the development and operation of this type of restaurant   For the tenant, designing and securing approval for the drive aisle presents a challenge that requires coordination with many parties, including the landlord, architect, adjacent businesses, and local planning authorities and building departments.

Use. Your lease should specifically state that you to operate a drive-thru. The following language is typical: "Tenant shall have the right to operate a drive-thru restaurant containing one drive-thru lane as shown on the site plan attached to this lease (and a pass-thru lane if required by any applicable laws, rules, or regulations)." The drive-thru lane and associated improvements may be part of the leased premises, or they may be part of the common area. If they are part of the common area, then you should have an irrevocable license for the exclusive use of the entire portion of the common area to be used for the drive-thru lane. In general, your lease should reserve the right to use any portions of the common area necessary to support the operation of a drive-thru restaurant. You should carefully review a title report and survey to be certain that the landlord owns the areas in question, that there is appropriate access to the adjacent public streets, and that no other party has any prior rights that might interfere with your use.

Due Diligence and Zoning Modifications. The first step in the due diligence process is to determine if local zoning codes permit a drive-thru to operate on the property you want to lease. Even if legally allowed, construction and operation of the restaurant will likely be subject to a series of conditions imposed by the local zoning authority (often following a public hearing), including the number of cars that must be able to be "stacked" in the drive-thru lane without impeding access to and from on-site spaces or backing up into the street, noise restrictions, trash pick-up and cleaning, and hours of operation. You may also be required to pay for street widening and the installation of a traffic light or other traffic control device. As part of your application for a zoning variance or conditional use permit, you will be required to submit a proposed site plan showing the entire site as it will appear following completion of construction. An example of a detailed site plan follows on the next page.

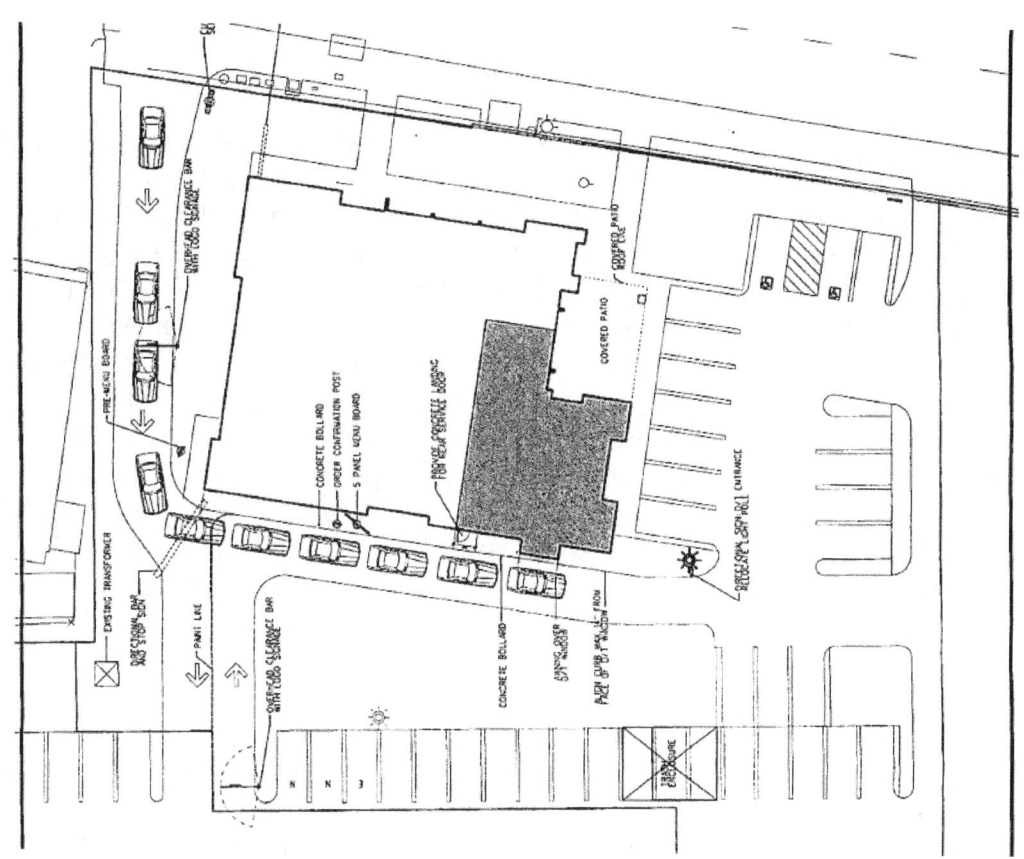

typical site plan for a drive-thru restaurant

Signage.   You should have the right to display in the common areas all appropriate directional signage, menu boards, and other signage associated with the drive-thru facility. You should also be permitted to display promotional materials within the drive-thru area, regardless of whether they are directly leased or part of the common area. This is especially important for franchise operations that are obligated to participate in franchisor-mandated advertising campaigns.

Repair Obligations.   The areas of a drive-thru that most often need repair are the electrical and mechanical elements of the speaker system and the menu board. Because these elements are connected to the inside of your restaurant, they usually include wires and controls in conduits and boxes placed beneath the driveway. The burden of paying for the repairs generally falls upon the party that constructed them, but the lease needs to identify the responsible party. If the underground conduit is sufficiently large or there is duplicate empty conduit, your repair of electrical and mechanical elements can often be done by running new wiring through the existing or duplicate conduit. Otherwise, the driveway may need to be excavated to repair the damaged components and this may disrupt your operations. Ask your architect if these steps make sense for your site; it may save you from having to close the drive-thru.

Conclusion

The irony of commercial leasing is that the more successful the business, the less likely that either the landlord or the tenant will have any reason to look at the lease after it has been signed. The lease is like the owner's manual to your car; unless a warning light goes off, you don't give it much thought. Also, most landlords act in a reasonable and responsible manner when faced with a potential problem. The lease may give your landlord a termination right, but most landlords prefer to help you stay in business. Your landlord does not want to spend the time and money required to find another tenant. Given all that, there is no need to beat yourself up if you don't get all of the changes to the lease that you want. Do your best, and then sit back and look at the lease as a whole. Ask yourself if, on balance, it is a fair agreement that generally meets your needs. Then consider the lease as one of the many building blocks of your restaurant. Ask yourself if, taken together, the lease, location, landlord, and all the other elements of the deal give you the confidence necessary to proceed. If so, then sign the lease and get started on the truly important work of designing a unique dining environment and a spectacular menu that will attract customers in droves!

Finally, a word about the care and feeding of your landlord. Everyone wants to feel like a special guest in a restaurant, to be greeted by name and shown to his or her regular table. Landlords are no different. Introduce the landlord to your staff and instruct them that he is a VIP. Of all the investments you make, none may pay more dividends than comping the landlord to a dinner or a nice bottle of wine now and then.

Bon Appetit!

Appendix A

Letter of Intent

The sample letter of intent that follows is based on an actual letter of intent for a shopping center restaurant lease negotiation, with the names and key economic terms changed. There is a lot that could be improved from a drafting standpoint, but these letters are usually cobbled together from previous deals by brokers and in-house representatives, with the goal of getting something signed as quickly as possible. The common theme is to "let the lawyers worry about it later." This is a first draft of a letter prepared by the landlord; the comments in bold type reflect the tenant's initial concerns.

RISKY DEVELOPMENT FUND IV
1 LOST PENSION PLAZA
NEW YORK, NEW YORK

SeaStuff , LLC
Attn: Ima Cook
1234 High Hopes Road
Palm Springs, California

Re: Restaurant Lease – Waterfront Mall, Palm Springs, CA

Dear Ms. Cook:

This letter will confirm the business terms for the lease (the "Lease") between Risky Development Fund IV and SeaStuff, LLC for the project (the "Project") known as Waterfront Mall at the northwest corner of Desert Way and Cactus Road in Palm Springs, California.

LANDLORD: Risky Development Fund IV

TENANT: SeaStuff, LLC

GUARANTOR: Ima Cook will personally guaranty the payment of all rent and the performance of all obligations under the Lease. **[There should be a limit on the amount of Tenant's liability.]**

PREMISES: The premises shall consist of approximately 7,000 square feet of restaurant space located in the building identified on Exhibit "A" attached hereto (the "Premises"). The exact size and dimensions are subject to final approval based on industry standards of space measurement acceptable to both parties. **[There are various methods of measuring premises, especially in multi-tenant buildings. Tenant should discuss this with its architect or space planner.]**

USE: Full-service seafood restaurant with beer, wine and liquor. Tenant agrees to open the Premises as a full-service seafood restaurant operating under the name "SeaStuff" in a manner consistent with Tenant's other SeaStuff restaurants in Southern California, and to continuously operate in such a manner for a period of three full lease years (except in the case of damage or destruction or other matters beyond Tenant's control, in which event Tenant shall have such time as is reasonably necessary to reopen.) After the third full lease year, no covenant of continuous operation is expressed or implied; provided, however, if Tenant ceases to operate for a continuous period of 90 days (except as provided in the immediately preceding sentence), then Landlord shall have the right to terminate the Lease unless Tenant **[or an assignee or subtenant]** reopens for business within 30 days following Landlord's notice of termination.

LEASE TERM: The primary lease term (the "Initial Term") will be 10 years, commencing on the Rent Commencement Date. **[Tenant would prefer a 5-year initial term.]**

OPTIONS: Tenant shall have the right to extend the term of the lease for 3 **[Tenant would like 4]** consecutive periods of 5 years each, at the rental rates set forth below.

CONTINGENCY PERIOD: Tenant shall have 90 days **[Tenant needs 120 -150 days]** from the date the Lease is fully executed to complete all due diligence investigations and inspections and to obtain all construction, operating and use permits and licenses. If any investigations or inspections reveal conditions that are unacceptable to Tenant, then Tenant may elect to terminate the Lease unless Landlord agrees to repair or mitigate such conditions. If Tenant, after diligent effort, is unable to obtain approvals for permits and licenses for its intended use, then Tenant may elect to terminate the Lease. **[Add Tenant's right to extend contingency period if all applications for permits and licenses have been verbally approved and Tenant is waiting for city to issue them.]**

POSSESSION DATE: The "Possession Date" shall be the later of (a) the date on which Landlord delivers the Premises to Tenant for build-out and fixturing with all Landlord Work completed (the "Delivery Date"), and (b) the date on which all Tenant contingencies are removed. **[There should be a limit on how long Tenant has to wait for the Delivery Date to occur. If the Delivery Date does not occur within 180 days following the removal of Tenant's contingencies, then Tenant may elect to either terminate the Lease or extend the Delivery Date. If Tenant elects to terminate the Lease, then Landlord will reimburse Tenant for Tenant's out-of-pocket expenses.]**

RENT COMMENCEMENT: Rent shall commence 180 days after the Possession Date.

ANNUAL GROSS RENT: The Annual Gross Rent (including all Taxes, CAM, and Insurance) shall initially be $120,000, paid in equal monthly installments of $10,000 per month, and shall increase annually, including during the Options, in accordance with the provisions below.

OPTION RENT: If Tenant elects to exercise its rights to extend the Initial Term, then the following Annual Gross Rent will be the contracted rates for each Option Period:

Option 1   (Years 11 – 15) $160,000
Option 2   (Years 16 – 20) $200,000
Option 3   (Years 21 – 25) $240,000

ANNUAL RENT ESCALATION: Annual Gross Rent shall increase by two percent (2%) per year on a cumulative and compounded basis.

PERCENTAGE RENT: Tenant agrees to pay Landlord percentage rent equal to five percent (5.0%) of its annual gross sales in excess of the sales breakpoint. The initial sales breakpoint shall be $3,000,000, and shall be increased annually by the same percentage as the Annual Gross Rent is increased (the "Sales Breakpoint"). **["Gross sales" means the total revenue derived from sales of food and beverages to customers, excluding refunds, sales taxes, off-site catering, sales of fixtures and equipment, insurance proceeds, credit card fees, bad debts for house accounts, the value of complimentary meals and meals sold to employees at a discount, charitable contributions, and gift certificates sold but not redeemed.]**

OPERATING EXPENSES: None.

REAL ESTATE TAXES: None.

RENTAL ABATEMENT: None.

PARKING: Tenant's employees and customers shall be allowed to park in all unreserved parking areas, subject to availability. **[Landlord shall provide not less than 36 spaces for non-exclusive use by Tenant's patrons, during Tenant's hours of operation, at no cost to Tenant or its patrons. These spaces will be located in the area identified as "Protected Parking Zone" on Exhibit "A" attached hereto. In addition, provision shall be made for additional parking spaces to accommodate overflow parking, as agreed upon between Landlord and Tenant. Landlord shall designate a non-reserved area for employee parking that will be provided at no charge to Tenant's employees.]**

TRASH SERVICE: Landlord shall provide Tenant with a convenient location for a dedicated trash compactor with service to be contracted for directly by Tenant. At Landlord's election, Landlord may provide a refrigerated holding area for Tenant's trash.

NATURAL GAS: Tenant shall contract directly with the gas company for individually metered service to its Premises.

UTILITIES: Landlord will provide the required utility service per Tenant's specifications at locations specified within the Premises per the attached Landlord work letter. Tenant shall contract for payment directly to the utility companies serving the Premises or reimburse Landlord monthly for utility usage costs. Meters or sub-meters will be provided and installed by Landlord, if not provided and installed by the utility company.

LANDLORD IMPROVEMENTS: Landlord shall perform such improvements to the Premises ("Landlord's Work") as shall be required in order to deliver the Premises to Tenant in accordance with Tenant's work letter (the "Work Letter") attached hereto as Exhibit "B."

TENANT IMPROVEMENTS: Except for Landlord's Work and the Contribution, Tenant shall be responsible for all costs associated with Tenant's improvements. Landlord shall have the reasonable right to approve Tenant's plans; provided, however, Landlord waives any objections to Tenant's standard interior trade dress.

CONTRIBUTION: In addition to Landlord's Work, Landlord agrees to provide Tenant with a cash allowance equal to One Million Dollars ($1,000,000) as the "Contribution". The Contribution shall be applied toward the cost of Tenant's improvements to the Premises Funds shall be distributed to Tenant according to the following schedule:

> 1/2 when Tenant finishes 50% of its construction; and
> 1/2 when Tenant opens to the public.

SIGNAGE: Tenant shall be entitled to place its prototypical signage and logo, to the maximum allowable legal limits, on all exterior and interior storefront elevations. The signage package and exterior storefront design shall be agreed to by Tenant and Landlord and attached as an exhibit to the Lease. Tenant shall provide Landlord with a preliminary plan indicating Tenant's signage package within sixty 60 days following the execution of this Letter of Intent for Landlord's consent. **[If Landlord erects any signage for the project on Desert Way, then Tenant will have the right to be included in a manner consistent with its size and position within the center.]**

.

NO BUILD ZONE: Landlord shall not allow the construction of any structure, or placement of any kiosk or other type of temporary or permanent structure, within 50 feet of Tenant's main entrance in any position that will reduce Tenant's visibility or cause to change the ingress of its customers or their vehicles.

RADIUS RESTRICTION: Tenant agrees not to open another full-service seafood restaurant **[under the name SeaStuff]** within five (5) miles of the Premises for the entire term of the lease.

EXCLUSIVITY: Tenant shall have the exclusive right to operate a full-service seafood restaurant at the Project. Tenant's exclusive shall not prohibit the operation of another restaurant having a floor area less than 3,000 square feet whose menu has not more than 5 seafood items, excluding sushi, and an average food check of less than $25.00 per person.

SUBLEASING AND ASSIGNMENT: Tenant shall have the right, without Landlord's consent, to assign the Lease or sublet the Premises to any corporation which is owned by or closely affiliated with Tenant, or to any subsidiary corporation of Tenant, Tenant's parent corporation, Guarantor, or to any corporation succeeding to substantially all the assets of Tenant as a result of a consolidation, merger, or sale, or to an corporation which acquires a majority of Tenant's other units.

[Tenant shall further have the right to assign the lease or sublet the Premises subject to Landlord's consent, which consent shall not be unreasonably conditioned, delayed, or withheld for any reason other than the demonstrated unsuitability of the proposed subtenant or assignee, as outlined in the Lease.]

AGREEMENT: Landlord and Tenant agree to negotiate in good faith the terms of a definitive lease for the Premises, incorporating the terms of this Letter of Intent. This Letter of Intent constitutes a summary of the negotiations to date and does not result in any contractual obligation by either party to the other and nothing in this Letter of Intent shall be construed as creating any rights in favor of or obligations burdening either party.

Appendix B

Work Letter

The attached work letter describes the work that the landlord is required to complete in the premises before delivering the space to the tenant. The tenant's work is not specifically described; to do so might create a situation where something is inadvertently omitted from both parties' work descriptions. To avoid this problem, the best practice is for the work letter to specify in detail the work to be performed by one party, and to state that the other party will perform all other work required in order to open and operate as a full-service restaurant in accordance with applicable law.

An architect prepared this work letter for a particular project. The specifications are only an example of what you might see in a typical lease. The technical nature of the description of the work should make you realize how important it is to involve an architect or contractor early in the lease negotiations.

Landlord's Work: Landlord shall perform the following work in the Premises and the Building at its sole cost and expense, in accordance with the terms of the Lease to which this Work Letter is attached.

Hazardous Materials. Provide environmentally clean Premises free from all hazardous materials. Current Phase I environmental report to be furnished by Landlord.

Structure. Provide structurally sound Premises, to include slab floors, columns, walls, ceilings and load-bearing elements and components. Landlord's design to provide for a live floor load of no less than _____ pounds per square foot. Complete seismic upgrade if required.

Floors. Provide level and flat floors, or subfloors ready for the installation of Tenant's finishing floor materials.

Walls. Provide perimeter walls and demising walls and adequate insulation to perimeter walls. Walls to be closed by Tenant after Tenant completes electrical and mechanical distribution.

Storefront and Entrances. Provide, at Tenant's option, either (i) a storefront and entrance to Premises in accordance with Tenant's storefront design and schematic space utilization plan, or (ii) a "Storefront and Entrance Allowance" that is representative of Landlord's cost of executing option (i).

Electrical. Provide 1000 amp, 240 volts, 3-phase electrical service to the Premises with distribution box at location determined by Tenant and ready for distribution. Provide meter or submeter.

Water. Provide a 2 ½" domestic water line stubbed to the Premises at location determined by Tenant and ready for distribution. Water line must maintain minimum of 60 lbs. of pressure. Provide meter or submeter.

Gas Service. Provide 2" gas line stubbed to Premises at location determined by Tenant and ready for distribution. Provide meter or submeter.

Sanitary Sewer. Provide one (1) four-inch (4") sanitary sewer line and one (1) four-inch (4") grease waste line stubbed to Premises at location determined by Tenant. This work shall include a grease trap for grease storage appropriately sized as where required by local governing authority. Combined sewers shall be a minimum of six inches (6") and all sanitary and waste lines shall have adequate inverts and slope to maintain sufficient flow rate. Provide sump pump and/or sewage lifts/ejectors if so required. Landlord shall pay any sewer connection charges.

Fire Protection. Provide sprinkler system with normal grid and head placement within the Premises with sufficient pressure and size to meet codes.

HVAC System. Provide sufficient HVAC to maintain a 70-74 degree Fahrenheit temperature throughout the Premises. HVAC should include outdoor air ventilation as required by code and be stubbed to Premises at location to be determined by Tenant. System shall be capable of supplying the kitchen make-up air, kitchen, bar and three dining room zones for a total of six (6) zones. Provide submeters if required. (Distribution of HVAC within the Premises is to be by Tenant at Tenant's expense.)

Exhaust and Venting. Provide shafts and ductwork to accommodate venting of all kitchen equipment, fresh air intake supply and make-up air system from exterior of Premises to the roof of the building in accordance with local codes. Venting of kitchen equipment through kitchen hood duct system from exterior of Premises to roof of building will include black iron, fire protection, roof curbs, and scrubber unit if required by applicable law or code and make-up air and exhaust fans as required by local code. Landlord will also provide vents for gas water heater and gas reheat units, toilet exhaust for all restrooms and a four-inch (4") plumbing vent. All vents, shafts, ductwork and exhaust shall be stubbed to Premises at locations to be determined by Tenant and shall be constructed in compliance with all applicable laws.

Telephone Service. Provide empty conduit from a telephone demarcation point.

Fire and Security Systems. Provide conduits from Premises to fire alarm annunciation, strobes and security system panel(s) to accommodate Tenant's connection to building fire alarm and security systems. Provide access to Building's emergency lighting power supply to accommodate Tenant's required emergency lighting requirements.

Appendix C

Construction Timeline

The attached timeline is a good template, but you will need to customize it for your particular deal.

Action	Time
Landlord provides plans and specifications for Premises ("Base Plans").	When LOI is signed.
Tenant provides rough drawings of desired improvements to Premises ("Preliminary Plans").	Within 30 days following the later of (1) lease execution, or (2) Landlord's delivery of Base Plans.
Landlord approves or disapproves Preliminary Plans.	Within 10 days following delivery of Preliminary Plans. Process of revising and reviewing Preliminary Plans continues until both sides are satisfied.
Tenant prepares final architectural drawings ("Final Plans").	Within 30 days following Landlord's final approval of Preliminary Plans.
Tenant submits Final Plans to government agencies for building permits ("Building Permits").	Within 10 days following Landlord's approval of Final Plans.
Landlord commences Landlord's Work.	Within 10 days following issuance of Building Permit.
Tenant commences Tenant's Work.	Within 10 days following completion of Landlord's Work.
Tenant applies to government agency for Certificate of Occupancy	Upon completion of Landlord's Work and Tenant's Work.
Tenant opens for business.	Within 10 days following issuance of Certificate of Occupancy.

Appendix D

CAM Exclusions

The attached list of items excluded from common area maintenance expenses is fairly standard and should not be objectionable to the landlord. As previously noted, there is no point to negotiating exclusions unless you take the time to review the annual expense statement provided by the landlord to make certain that it includes only allowable expenses.

The following costs and expenses are commonly excluded from CAM Expenses:

1.   The cost of construction or reconstruction of any portion of the Shopping Center;

2.   The cost of improvements deemed to be a capital expense, or the cost of renting equipment that would be a capital expense if purchased;

3.   Any cost to repair Common Area to the extent covered by insurance or warranty;

4.   Depreciation;

5.   Interest, late charges, and penalties on any CAM expenses, except to the extent resulting from the tenant's failure to timely pay its share of CAM expenses;

6.   Attorneys' fees and costs;

7.   The cost of improvements or services that do not benefit the tenant;

8.   Expenses incurred in connection with leases with any existing or prospective tenants;

9.   Amounts payable under mortgages, deeds of trust, or ground leases;

10.   Costs or expenses of securing governmental approvals to construct or operate the Shopping Center;

11.   Costs and expenses of investigating, removing, maintaining or monitoring any hazardous material, (except minor oil or gasoline leakage from cars) or any costs and expenses of complying with applicable laws relating to hazardous materials;

12.   Costs that are reimbursable to the landlord by tenants as a result of provisions contained in their specific lease, such as excessive use of utilities;

13.   Management fees, administrative fees, overhead or profit;

14.   Any compensation paid to clerks, attendants or other persons in commercial concessions operated by the landlord;

15.   Advertising and promotional expenditures;

16.   Costs incurred in operating and maintaining the Shopping Center's parking facilities if the Landlord charges for parking;

17.   Wages, salaries or other compensation paid to any employee above the grade of property manager; and

18.   The cost or rental value of vacant space in the Shopping Center, or space provided for maintenance, management, administrative, or security functions.

About the Author

Alan Aronson is a native of Seattle, Washington. He worked his way down the Pacific Coast in search of the sun, stopping in Palo Alto to earn a bachelors degree in Economics from Stanford and then continuing south to earn a law degree at UCLA. Before his recent retirement, Alan practiced law in Los Angeles for twenty-five years, primarily in the field of restaurant and general retail leasing. His restaurant clients included regional and national chains with concepts ranging from fine dining to fast food.